THE TAO
OF NOW

THE TAO
OF NOW

Daniel Skach-Mills

K ℰ𝕟 A 𝐫𝐧𝐨𝐥𝐝 B 𝐨𝐨𝐤𝐬 LLC
Portland, Oregon

Library of Congress Control Number: 2008927444

Published by KenArnoldBooks, LLC

ISBN: 978-0-615-32124-0

The Dow that rises and falls,
gains and loses,
is not the eternal Tao.

—*D. Skach-Mills*

INTRODUCTION

Perusing a local bookstore, I was surprised to find little on the Taoism shelf except the usual plethora of commentaries on and translations of the *I Ching*, Lao Tzu's *Tao Te Ching*, and the writings of Chuang Tzu. The only other works were a book of daily meditations based on Taoist aphorisms, and a primer on Eastern philosophy tucked between Benjamin Hoff's bestsellers, *The Tao of Pooh* and *The Te of Piglet*.

I did find some books with "Tao" in the title in the "Self-Improvement" section. This struck me as incongruous, since realizing Tao means waking up from the illusory self (or ego) that constantly seeks to improve, enhance, and solidify itself. Sadly, some of these texts reduced the Tao to a mere selling point, just one more "way" (Tao, in Chinese, means "way" or "path") for the ego to get what it wants.

What I was unable to find were contemporary works that captured the same spontaneous style and spirit of the Taoist classics. This led me to wonder why. For if the eternal Tao is indeed eternal, then wouldn't that same spirit which moved Lao Tzu and others to write over two-thousand years ago still be alive, well, and as available today as it was then? And if so, what might it look like? what might it be saying?

The book you are holding is the answer life gave me to these questions. It began, quite unexpectedly, with some insights I jotted down while facilitating a workshop on present-moment awareness for the local Unitarian Church. Other realizations grew out of my work as a volunteer docent at Lan Su Chinese Garden in Portland, Oregon. Over time, these jottings and musings morphed into a poetic style, and the insights increased, often to five or six per day. Within three months, my notepad was filled with almost one-hundred verses.

Those familiar with the *Tao Te Ching* might look at this collection and wonder: *So what is this exactly? A translation? Version? Adaptation? Interpretation?* It's actually none of these. The work appears to be an incarnation of something ancient, yet new—ancient in that, for millennia, poets have been penning words that point to the larger Reality; new, because the verses incorporate names, images, and allusions that will be familiar to the contemporary reader.

Some may be surprised to discover that the word *Tao* does not appear anywhere in the book except in the title, epigraph, and this introduction. There is a reason for this. According to the late Asia scholar and self-proclaimed "spiritual entertainer" Alan Watts, "the Tao is available to our perception when we are fully in the present moment," or the Now. In short, if this book reopens the door of your awareness to the Now, it has done its job, and realizing Tao will take care of itself.

Timeless as the classic Taoist texts are, there are challenges facing us today that no one, not even Lao Tzu, could have imagined in the sixth century BC. The contemporary urgency for a consciousness and heart revolution is no longer an option if the planet, and humanity as a species, are to survive. *The Tao of Now* may help to shift our consciousness by holding up mirrors both to the individual's mind-made sense of self, and to our culture's mind-dominated social, religious, and political structures.

If you find intellectual answers here it is purely accidental. The verses are aimed not at your thinking mind, but at re-awakening that part of you that already knows everything the text is saying. As such, it is more like remembering what you have always known, rather than a fresh piece of mind-candy.

Finally, please note that I have arranged the collection in eighty-one verses or chapters, the same as Lao Tzu's *Tao Te Ching*. In Chinese numerology, nine is a propitious number because it is a pun on the word "forever." Nine times nine, totaling eighty-one, is doubly propitious, and could (in my imagination, anyway) be pointing to "forever times forever," or the eternal Tao. I have retained this arrangement as a way of honoring both the ancient text and the numerological tradition.

My hope is that these writings will stand as a contemporary witness that the eternal Tao is alive, well, and waiting for anyone who takes the time to unplug, unwind, and listen with their whole Being.

—*Daniel Skach-Mills*

One

A stream doesn't come to a rock
and have a crisis—*Which way do I go?*
Which way do I go?!
It simply flows around.

The organs in your body
—stomach, heart, liver—
all know what to do without
your having to think.

This Intelligence is like a shoreless ocean.
The human mind: a drop of rain.
The drop contains the ocean,
the ocean contains the drop,
but is infinitely beyond it.
It manifests, permeates,
and sustains all things.
It pours forth the changeless,
silent, formless space
within which the world of form
ceaselessly comes and goes.

Some call this space: *Emptiness.*
Vastness. The present moment.
Others call it the *Now.*

Simply being,
a rare few say nothing.
And they have revealed
everything.

Two

Turn your attention to the Now,
and thinking gives way to Being.

When thinking gives way to Being,
there's a felt sense of oneness with life.

A felt sense of oneness with life radiates Presence.
Presence emanates from the Source.

Right about now, the mind will ask:
*But how do I incorporate the Source
into my life?*

You don't. It's impossible.
That would be like attempting to pour
the universe into a shot glass.
Try all you want,
how are you going to get
drunk with love on that?

Empty the watered-down life
your mind's been serving you
into the Source. Then, set aside
the glass.

The Now is the no-name-tag party
you've been throwing
and inviting yourself to
since before you were
even born.

Three

Being is like a forest.

It has no need of doorways
because it is its own portal.
It allows entry anywhere
without opening a single latch.

Wherever you walk
the deep roots are there,
but you cannot see them.

Getting lost in these trees
means the end of circling
around and around
what you've always been.

Four

A developer walking through a forest
sees a potential resort.
A contractor driving past
sees hundreds and hundreds of acres
of new and expensive homes.

The poet sees a poem;
the lumberman: X number of board feet;
the religious person: the dark night of the soul.

A man awakened to the Now
builds nothing out of thought,
eschews superfluous words,
experiences darkness
as the source of all knowing.

Looking, he doesn't see anything.
He simply steps out of the way
and lets seeing see.

Five

A gunshot startles a thousand birds.
A thought erupts into a thousand emotions.

The sky's vastness embraces everything.
The tree doesn't confuse
the coming and going of birds
with what it is.

Stay rooted like that,
moving only if you have to,
making *here* your only word.

Six

Spiritual paths are like lovers:
the true ones aren't always good looking;
the good looking ones
aren't always true.

Living in an alpine valley,
a person comes to believe
that the path to fulfillment and happiness
lies on the other side of the mountain.
The person living opposite
believes the same.

Now where do you go?

Remain where you are,
and arrive without departing.
Remain where you are not,
and there is only the One—
still, silent, complete unto itself,
it is like the mountain that sees
all of its sides at once
without having to look.

Seven

You can't turn a stone into a fish
by throwing it into the water.
You can't turn a stick into a bird
by tossing it repeatedly into the air.

Only a fool tries to make flowers grow
by pulling up on the stems.

The truth that can be bent by words
isn't the deep truth.
The truth that can be twisted
is itself a part of the lie.

What's real remains true to itself
even in the midst of human chaos.
No truth can add insight to it,
no untruth detract.

Steady, constant,
it never shouts, imposes, insists. Why?
Because it doesn't have to.
Because it's all there is.

Eight

The Now is easy.
People make it hard.

The Now is here.
People put it "there."

The ego is always wanting
this or that to complete itself.
The Now is always
wanting *this*.

The mind is forever seeing itself
at the center of everything.
The Now is forever,
seeing.

Nine

Move to the left,
and you create right.

Move up,
you create down.

Cling to the so-called "good,"
and evil appears.

Every move
manifests its opposite.

Therefore,
live solely from the center.

Be still.

Ten

To say that the pendulum
has swung too far in one direction
and now must swing back
is to deny that the clock is broken.

Let go of good versus evil
in favor of balance and harmony,
and what you call good
will naturally flow out of that.

Step out of the swing
between *this* or *that*
and you won't even
have to try.

Eleven

The human mind
is like a potato ricer—
put the world in,
push down the plunger of thought,
and out comes the oneness
separate and fragmented
through a hundred holes.

To know the potato as it is,
put aside the ricer.
To know life as it is,
put aside the mind.

Twelve

Rain fills the barrel
without straining or striving.
The river gets to where it's going
without once stopping to think.

"Is the glass half empty or half full?"
is just another mind question.
The water inside never judges itself
as more or less, muddy or clear,
too hot or too cold.

It doesn't even care.

Thirteen

Mind gives birth to ego.
Ego gives birth to wanting
to become something.

Complete in itself,
Being doesn't grasp at
or push away anything.

Can the air inhale more
of what it already is?
Can a bird flying freely
divest itself of the sky?

Be what you truly are,
and all wanting ceases.

Relinquish being something,
and become everything.

Fourteen

The ego is like a bat.
The mind? Its poor attempt
at sonar.

The bat bounces sonar off its surroundings
to determine where it is in relation
to life and the world.
The ego continually
enlists the mind
to do the same.

For lack of a better term,
we'll call this mind bouncing:
endless self-referencing.

What do I think of this? of that?
Is this getting me what I want?
Are people here noticing me?
Appreciating me?
He drives a Porsche;
but I'm more spiritual.

Flap, flap, flap.

Like a bat,
the ego is always homing in
on whatever it can consume or hang on to.
Its view of life and the world
turns everything upside down.
Were it to stop hanging itself up like this,
the mind couldn't take off.
It would stop flying around
altogether.

Fifteen

Struggling to make it to the top.
Struggling to avoid hitting bottom.
It's all the same.

The elevator
in an office building
moves up and down.
Riding it either way,
you're still closed
inside a box.

Step off where there is no floor.
That way, there's nothing
to carry you toward
or away from
anything.

Sixteen

The average person thinks mastery of life
means grabbing it by the balls
and making it do what you want.
This is how an entire civilization
renders itself impotent,
and makes the planet sterile.
This is how day-to-day life becomes
a constant ache to walk through.

Because the person who's realized the Now
doesn't dominate, she's seen as weak.
Because she doesn't overpower,
she appears powerless.
Because she refuses to manipulate and use,
she's viewed as useless.
Because she feels no need to be "more than,"
she's judged by others as less.

Never pushing down those around her
in order to get ahead,
she's labeled as having no ambition.
Relinquishing control over people and situations,
she's written off as being ineffective.
Free from struggling to get to the top,
she no longer cares if the world sees her
as living at the bottom.
Content with letting others compete for first place,
she's always perfectly content.

Thus she masters life by being life;
masters the Now by being her self;
masters herself by being the Now.

Seventeen

The way up the ladder
is also the way down.
The doorway in
is also the doorway out.

Those who embody the Now
embody openness.
Those who don't are like bees
confined in a jar:
after a few hours they won't fly free,
even when the lid's removed.

Adjusted to captivity,
they view life through
the container's distorted glass,
but think they're seeing it
as it really is.

Were the jar to break,
they'd swear that death had come
and taken them to some other side.

They'd look around
and call it "heaven."

Eighteen

Step back from a difficulty
to think about it,
and you've already stepped back
from the solution.

Focus on the words
to find the next stanza,
and you've already hidden yourself
from the poem.

The mind is clever.
Being is wise.

Mind reacts, judges, rejects.
Being does or doesn't respond.

The mind separates itself from life,
and then struggles to think
of what to do.

Being *is* life,
responding to itself.

Use thinking,
but don't be used by it.

Be Being,
and answers arise spontaneously
out of the questions
like bubbles out of water.

Nineteen

A boat needs the water,
but water doesn't need the boat.
A traveler uses a road,
but the road doesn't need the traveler.
It gets to where it's going
whether anyone follows it or not.

The Now is like that—
there for anyone to use,
but not using or needing
anyone or anything
in order to be
what it is.

Twenty

Consume bitterness:
you are tasting your self.
Make love:
you are loving your self.
Witness war:
you are watching your self.
Feel the wind:
you are feeling your self.
Smell sewage:
you are smelling your self.
Enjoy music:
you are hearing your self.
Listen to silence:
you are being your self.

Morning, noon, and night
the awakened person lives like this,
checking the window to see
if she is raining, sunny,
dark.

Because she doesn't *have* a life,
but *is* life, she lives without fear.
Because she lives *as* the world,
rather than *in* the world,
she has compassion for every being.
Because her heart is centered in the Now,
she feels no need to comprehend it.
She simply lets it be her self.

41

Twenty-One

Oak remains oak,
no matter what you carve it into.
Granite remains granite,
even after becoming a house.

Stay true to what you are
and no matter what form the moment takes
you'll be at peace.

Root yourself in what is,
and your days will spread out
like the far-reaching limbs
on an ancient inexhaustible tree
from which one person
will hew a walking stick
another, posts and lintels
still another, a mantel.

Branch out everywhere
without moving anywhere,
and you will be what sages call:
support for the journey;
a doorway for others;
the center of what it means
to be home.

Twenty-Two

Pick up a hammer to use it.
Put it down when you're through.

Use your own mind like that,
as a tool rather than a self,
and you'll no longer
be wielding what nails you
to building yourself up
or knocking others down.

You won't even have to lay
a foundation for peace.

Twenty-Three

A walled garden thrives
in the midst of a bustling city.

Inside, there's the tranquil water
and the silence and the flowers
unfolding in stillness.

Outside: honking buses and motorists
and the cacophony of squealing brakes.

Traffic noise, mental noise—
both are irrelevant.

Remain centered in the Now,
and all the bumper-to-bumper thinking
exits immediately to the outskirts.

Abide as stillness
in the midst of the world's drivenness,
and be the free way
all the others are looking for.

Twenty-Four

The scent of one blossoming Osmanthus tree
fills the entire neighborhood.
The aroma from a single one of its flowers
wafts through every room.

Those who notice the fragrance, notice.
Those who don't, don't.

Readiness is everything.
Without it, who can recognize
that sweet perfume permeating
within and without?

Serene, silent,
the tree wants nothing,
asks nothing.

Ignore it, curse it, praise it,
the scent remains untouched.

Be like that—
your fragrance drifting every direction
without discriminating,
never withholding life from life.

Twenty-Five

Can you tend a garden
without turning deer and insects
into enemies?

Can you drive a vehicle in winter
without making a menace
of snow?

Can you plan a gathering
without planning on others
to execute and follow your plans?

Practice what's easy first.
Then, when illness comes,
and finally death,
you'll be ready
to let go of plans,
drive straight ahead,
attend to what's being eaten away
without bitterness.

When life moving in
and out of itself
is all you can see,
then you are at peace
with everything.

Twenty-Six

A spider frees her web of leaves
by cutting away the sticky strands.
An awakened person
frees her mind of clutter
by cutting away sticky thoughts.

In this way,
both remain one with Oneness,
abiding peacefully at the center,
being nourished by
whatever comes.

Twenty-Seven

Without earth to grow the wheat field,
where is the cake?

Without water to moisten
the pastry dough,
where is the pie?

Without heat to bake the loaf,
where is the bread?

Without air to nourish the body,
where is the one who eats?

The wise woman knows
there is no self
separate from everything else.

Simple, expansive,
she moves through life as life,
peering deeply into what is.

Having stepped forever
beyond inner and outer,
she sees her body
everywhere.

Twenty-Eight

The water flowing inside
hears the water flowing outside,
and a man runs to urinate.

The breast milk flowing inside
hears the baby crying outside,
and a woman begins to lactate.

Inner and outer? Illusions.
Separation of anything from anything else? False.
Thirst and hunger for the divine? Misguided.

The sooner you realize
your self to be the eternal Oneness
pouring itself out
and drinking itself in,
the sooner you'll be what slakes
the parched prayers
of the world.

Twenty-Nine

When people lose touch with the Now,
the mind takes over.
When the mind takes over,
not-knowing is feared.

When not-knowing is feared,
death becomes an enemy,
forms are clung to as a way
to relieve anxiety,
and the balance between form
and formlessness is lost.

When balance is lost,
people flee from mystery.
When people flee from mystery,
fundamentalism appears.

Thirty

The Now never forgets a name
because it labels nothing.
It never forgets a face
because it's always
meeting itself.

The teaching here is simple:
forgetting is remembering;
unknowing: learning.

Some call it sacred;
others: ignorant and profane.
Both fail the course.

What's holy or not holy here
wouldn't even know.

Thirty-One

An educator pumps the student
full of information.
A spiritual teacher empties out
to reveal what's already there.

The educator adds.
The teacher removes.

She is like the autumn wind
that strips away more and more each day
until the limbs of the tree
are denuded and laid bare.
She slowly scatters who and what
the person thought they were
in a hundred different directions.

Wordless, but powerful,
ungraspable, but felt,
the student recognizes in her
the space between his own branches
that was always there.

Thirty-Two

There's nothing here
that you don't already know.
There's nothing here to get
that you don't already have.

All I can do is laugh
when the billowing smoke tells me
it can't see the fire!

Open the windows,
let in fresh air,
see through the mind's haze,
clear out of your own way.

Talking about the Now
is like discussing heat
on a freezing winter's night.
No matter how many words
you rub together,
you're still out in the cold.

Be like the wood
that longs to feel
and be the flame,
rather than just thinking
or talking about it.

Thirty-Three

You will never come to know your self
through intellectual knowledge.

You cannot acquire like an object
what it is you already are.

That would be like the sun
seeing its own light shining on the earth
and saying:

I want to get some of that.

Thirty-Four

If you think light is the solution,
you're still sitting in darkness.
If you think darkness is the problem,
you haven't yet realized the light.

To grasp what I'm saying:
stop grasping.
To kindle what I'm referring to:
stop lighting and relighting
the smoldering wick of your mind.

The wick's short-lived.
The candle that houses it melts.
Let the breath within these words
blow it out, once and for all.

Extinguish the movement
that keeps rubbing thoughts
together into a self,
and illumination bursts
spontaneously into flame
without even striking a match.

Thirty-Five

The only word "I" loves
better than itself is "not"—
that, not this
us, not them
me, not you
there, not here
past, not present
later, not Now.

Why does the I postpone
and fear the Now?

Because the I is not.
Because the I is the not
that the Now unties.

Thirty-Six

A spiritual seeker is like a kite flyer—
the pull toward the heavenly Source
becomes confused with flimsy paper and twine.
Techniques aimed at achieving
a higher and loftier altitude
distance the person from where
they already are.

Thus when the kite ascends, they ascend.
When it dips, veers, gets tangled in trees,
the person feels lost,
anxious, depressed.

All this is better known
as being strung along
by the mind.

Unable to let go of the string,
the seeker believes proficiency
at flying the kite is necessary
before he or she can look up
and see the sky.

Thirty-Seven

When the mind first hears about the Now
it conjures up an image,
then sets out to find it
as if it were a thing.

It's like a useless hound
pursuing the scent of its own tracks
around a large tree in the snow.
Circling, year after year,
the only thing it finds
is itself.

Can a foot step toward its own toes?
Can a hand reach for its own fingers?
Can boiling water scald itself,
a television watch itself?
Can a fork stab its own tines?

A stupid hunter cuts down the tree
and the dog heads for the next trunk.
An educated man storms off
and buys another dog.
The woman who is awake
leaves the dog where it is,
and gives up hunting
altogether.

Thirty-Eight

The mind is like the dog
that lives in the next yard.
Faced with nothing to occupy itself,
it yelps incessantly.

Attempting to locate the owner is useless.
Try as you might, there's no shutting it up.

When you're away,
neighbors tell you it's quiet.
Here, it barks.

Awake, it's silent.
Drifting towards sleep,
the racket's unrelenting.

Walk by where it lives,
and ten minutes later
it's still yapping about what's passed.
Allowed to run free,
whatever street you head down
it's coming toward you.

Stuck in its own small yard,
it's both safe and discontent.
It thinks it owns the entire neighborhood.
It trusts its own noise to protect it
from the silent intruder
it doesn't know.

Thirty-Nine

Small dogs tend to be yappers.
Big dogs doze and drool.

A large dog can deter an intruder
simply by sleeping on the porch.
At rest, but highly alert,
he growls as a stranger approaches
without even opening his eyes.

The tiny dog barks wildly,
runs inside and pees on the rug,
then hides under the table
and shakes.

The mind, being small,
makes a lot of noise because
it lives in constant fear.

Presence, being large,
does everything without doing.

There is never a mess
to clean up afterwards.

Forty

A teensy mouse
enters a spacious room
through openings,
large or small.

A tiny key unlocks
an enormous door.

A one-inch nail
joins together measurements
infinitely greater than itself.

A mere three-lettered "Yes"
in response to what is
opens into the infinity
of Now.

Contentment with being small
amid the great things
of this world.

This is the big-and-little
known secret.

Forty-One

When true creativity moves,
egoic thinking steps out of the way.
When thinking steps out of the way,
so does the I.

When the I steps out of the way,
hours pass, unnoticed.
When hours pass unnoticed
the I wonders where
the time went.

When the I disappears,
time disappears.

Forty-Two

A writer weaves a central character
into a mind-made story.
The ego weaves a mind-made story
into a central character.

Conflict, drama, denouement—
the events that make up the story are fact.
The self your mind keeps authoring
from the mental narrative
about the events
is fiction.

This is why the awakened person
has shelved being the main character;
is through trying to find himself
within the narrow margins
of his own mentally penned-in story.
Having recognized the protagonist
as inseparable from his mind's narration,
he skips to the end as quickly as possible
so he can be done with it
and close the book.

Completely off the page now,
the author he loves most
hasn't written a thing,
or published a single word.

He knows he's just another pseudonym
this ghost writer's been using,
volume after empty volume,
for a hundred-billion years.

Forty-Three

The person awakened to the Now
is like a good pot of tea—
strong, but not biting,
smooth, but not weak,
she brings people together,
permeates the entire room with fragrance
without even trying,
embodies the One Source that fills
an infinite variety of cups.

This is why people relax in her presence:
because she brings what's been
gathered on the heights
down to where people can taste it;
pours herself freely into emptiness,
which is why those around her
experience being filled.

Ask, and she'll tell you
her job is easy.
She simply lets whatever comes
brew into what it is.

Forty-Four

Wearing the shirt isn't more important
than putting it on or taking it off.

Drinking the water isn't more important
than pouring it into and picking up the glass.

Getting what you want out of the cupboard
doesn't deserve more attention
than opening and closing the doors.

Reaching the other side of the room
isn't more critical than the steps
it takes to get there.

Reduce life to a means to an end,
and you'll reach the end
having missed your life.

Give equal attention to every action,
no matter how small,
and whatever you come
into contact with
will be awakened
to the Now.

Forty-Five

Find the Now
by not finding it—that way,
it can never be lost.

Enter the Now
by not entering—that way,
you're never outside.

The you that's seeking the Now
will never find it.
The you who keeps
entering and leaving
entering and leaving
needs to get rid of the door.

This is how it is:
try all you want,
there's no moving
toward or away from
what's always here.

Forty-Six

Mystical "union"
first requires a belief
in mythical separation.

Mythical separation
then requires a belief
in the religion that created it
to bind the person back.

All in all,
it's like traveling
to the other side of the world
to buy a map from a man
who claims he can get you home
to where you already live.

Forty-Seven

Words about God are not God.
Definitions of the Now
are not the Now.

A man opens a dictionary,
cuts out the word *silence*
and tapes it to his ear
cuts out the word *wind*
and tapes it to his cheek
cuts out *honey*
and places it on his tongue
rose, and hangs it
under his nose
God, and holds it
before his eyes.

Then he wanders through the world,
wondering why he feels dead
rather than alive.

Stuck to words and labels,
he tries to find meaning in meanings.
Thus he is already twice removed
from life.

He is like a photographer
who's so busy looking
through his view finder
that he misses the actual trip;
who knows his own journey
only through the small four-by-six-inch prints
he looks at when he gets home.

Forty-Eight

How can you tell when a civilization
has lost touch with the Now?
When interpretations of holy texts
keep people looking to the past
for future deliverance.
When ten-thousand spiritual titles
line the bookstore shelves,
but the planet is dying
and the people remain lost.

Shelve the Now,
and spirituality becomes an industry
no different from any other.
It creates a market by convincing people
that they need something in order
to complete themselves.
It turns dissatisfaction with the past
into wanting change and success in the future,
thus overlooking the always available
completeness of the Now.
Once this is accomplished,
selling people what they already have
(and therefore don't need)
is simple and guaranteed.

Look—the ego uses spirituality
the way it uses everything else:
as a tool for self-enhancement;
as reinforcement against the demolition
that true spirituality is.

Forty-Nine

You'll never realize your own sacredness
by clinging to it in others,
no matter how holy they are.

That's like trying to find out
where it is you're standing
by looking under the shoes
of the person next to you:
the holiness has to keep stepping aside
so that you can stand where it was.
This can go on forever—
people sidestepping their own divinity,
turning themselves into followers.

Realize there's no stepping into sacredness
because there's no stepping out of it,
and all duality ends.

Be like an ancient mountain:
dark on one side, light on the other,
it gives rise to the polarities
but isn't affected by them.
In this way, it is like the Now—
firm, unshakable, rooted in itself.
No one had to design or build it.
No one can remember when
it wasn't there.

Fifty

I'm not Christian.
I'm not not Christian.
I'm not Hindu.
I'm not not Hindu.
I'm not Muslim.
I'm not not Muslim.
Not Taoist.
Not not Taoist.
Not Buddhist.
Not not Buddhist.
Not American.
Not not American.

Live as the Now,
and all the labels drop away.
Let all the labels drop away,
and movement becomes
as natural as a river,
as mapless as wind.

Simply love what's true
more than you love what's false,
and the truth effortlessly appears.
It's like an ocean that was always there
surrounding you on every side.
Struggling to swim toward
or away from it
is the biggest waste of energy
in the world.

Fifty-One

Can you stand
humble and upright,
like a garden stake
that does nothing?

Can you let things grow
at their own pace,
silently providing your support?

Can you remain hidden at the center,
while what's planted around you
flourishes?

Can you be the way
rather than showing the way,
allowing what's already there
to unfold and manifest itself?

If only religions were like this:
earth-based, allowing,
planted in the Now;
attracting a natural following
without leading;
falling away silently
after their work is done.

Fifty-Two

Hollyhocks spire
from a crack in the sidewalk.
Ferns cascade from a chink
in a garden wall.

Nothing good comes
from forcing something
to happen or not happen.
Nothing is further from the truth
than the mind continually thinking
life wouldn't get done without it.

How do you know when the mind
is forcing things to happen or not happen?
When agencies have to be formed
to protect the environment
and defend the natural world.
When people are conditioned to believe
that they can make their lives bloom endlessly
into whatever it is they want
in a world that's impermanent.

Trust life to sow and complete you
the way a seed's sown by the wind.
The small cracks between your thoughts
are the only soil the Now needs
to plant you in what you are.

Fifty-Three

Psychological fear
gives rise to accumulation.
Accumulation gives rise
to psychological fear.

The mind is like a cup
afraid of its own emptiness.
Wealth, possessions, status, knowledge,
it fills itself with what it knows
to quell the anxiety,
then fears the loss of what
it's accumulated
to buffer itself from pain.

Ten-thousand teachers, authors,
and others will show you how
to keep patching the cracks
and replenishing the cup
so that you can get a new
and better handle on life.

If and when you've had
your fill of this,
pour them out
into the Now,
the one hand open enough
to shatter the grip
that both cup
and handle
have on you.

Cease fearing
the loss of the known,
and the unknown
will hold no fear.

Fifty-Four

Get a grip on yourself,
and the Now slips
through your fingers.

Go "out of your mind,"
and instantly you
become sane.

Living in sanity.
Living insanity.

The tiniest space
changes everything.

Fifty-Five

A woman succeeds
in getting her act together;
but she's still living an act.

A therapist works with a client
on changing his script at mid-life;
but he's still living a script.

This is why we call them:
life *stages*.

Being in the Now
means forgetting all your lines,
missing all your cues,
relinquishing center stage,
closing opening night
and leaving the theater,
never to return.

Acting without acting,
reciting without rehearsing,
it's like the curtain
going up and going down
all at the same time.

Fifty-Six

The Now is like a movie screen;
the mind: a projector.

People forget the screen
and confuse themselves with the movie.
They get caught up in whatever drama's playing,
and think it's who they are.
When that happens,
there's laughing one minute
and crying the next.

Be like the screen
that accepts whatever's appearing,
but remains what it is.
Empty, subtle,
it's the constant background
upon which the mind's theatrics
play themselves out.
It lets all the titles and credits roll over it
without clinging to a single one.

When the show's over
and the curtain closes,
it relinquishes all the roles
and lets the stars fade
so that the real lights
can come on.

Fifty-Seven

Resting in the Now,
things no longer serve any purpose.
Abiding in the Now,
tomorrow loses all its importance.

What does it mean that things
no longer serve any purpose?
Stop trying to pin down
happiness, identity, and security
in the world of shifting forms,
and things quite naturally take on
their proper functions.

What does it mean that tomorrow
loses all importance?
No longer looking to the future
to complete yourself, the Now
spontaneously appears.

Step back
off the tiny porch of the self
into where you actually live.
Then the world's free
to deliver or not deliver
whatever it wants.

When nobody's living
at the old address,
what arrives or doesn't arrive
doesn't really matter.

Fifty-Eight

Stepping out of the Now,
a culture steps into ego.
Stepping into ego
it takes more than it gives;
consumes disproportionately to its size;
pursues self-satisfaction relentlessly,
and so is never satisfied;
sees obesity become epidemic.

All this because the ego
is always seeking *more*.

When the poor and hungry appear,
those in power claim there simply
isn't enough to go around.
Ego-based technologies
that exploit the natural world
to produce even more
inevitably arise.

When a way of life
is treated as inviolable
and not to be questioned,
the people will be led to seek solutions
in all the wrong places.

Starved for the Now,
they will eat themselves,
quite literally,
out of house and home.

Fifty-Nine

What's changeless sees what changes.
What's still sees what moves.

Can you synthesize your senses into one sense,
the way rain becomes a stream,
and a stream becomes a river,
and a river an ocean
that takes everything in?
Can you feel your own body's
subtle energy so completely
that this, rather than thinking,
becomes the source of all your action,
the ground of your identity?

Tasting a sound,
listening to a fragrance.
Don't think about it!
Do it!

Like sunlight soundlessly
touching a shiny brass bell,
every eye in the room
that's struck by it,
rings.

Sixty

Does the tree struggle to forgive the wind
for snapping off its branches?
Does the lake strive to absolve the hand
for breaking its surface with stones?

The egoic self is like a backpack;
human grudges: rocks.
Fill the pack, and you are constantly
leaning backwards, out of the Now
and into the past.

Pull out each rock,
toss it away,
and new ones replace the old
before you can zip it shut.

This is why the realized person
leaves the pack by the side of the trail:
so she can move
through the world with ease.
So she can use the energy
that would have been spent
on forgiving,
for giving.

Sixty-One

The female gives birth from the inside out.
The tiniest seed does the same.

Thus the inner is the mother of the outer;
the outer: a reflection of what's inside.

If a culture is filled with noise, drivenness,
and a polluted view of the world on the inside,
the outside will look the same.
If a civilization's internal climate is out of balance,
the external climate will be thrown off as well.

When craftsmanship gives way
to easier and faster and genuine imitation,
the people are no longer dovetailed
with the Now.

When the foundations of buildings
are facades—built to look like stone,
but aren't—the nation is already
collapsing from within.

Sixty-Two

No war is civil.
The first casualty is always the truth.
The first to be taken prisoner
are those who wage it.

Let your brain become a battlefield,
and you'll be at war forever.
Turn your thoughts into enemies,
and you'll be shooting down others
as well as yourself.
Treat your mind as mined,
and you'll never take
a single step in peace.

Conned into continual conflict.
This is how pure awareness
gets conscripted for a lifetime
into the ego's service.

Sixty-Three

Sun Tzu said:
To subdue the enemy
without fighting
is the highest skill.

Higher by far, I say,
is the ability to subdue
your own mind,
which creates both the enemy
and the fighting
in the first place.

Sixty-Four

When military language
permeates a culture—

when *fighting climate change*
persistently pummels
changing how we live

when *battle against cancer*
repeatedly slays
regimen for health

when *waging war on terror*
consistently camouflages
the *terror of waging war*—

that culture is already
at war with itself.

Desire and aversion,
conflict and fear—
words of war
turn into
death sentences.

Sixty-Five

A world power's currency is like a horny penis:

*Why should I be getting so little here at home
when I could be getting more over there?*

Straight as a flag pole, off it goes
to screw a weaker country.

"Then the flag follows the currency,
and the troops follow the flag."

Sixty-Six

A nation's flag is shaped like a box.
This is no coincidence.

The few who reach high enough
to peer over the edge
will incur the wrath of the many.
The one who steps out altogether
will be written off as mad.
Should she return
and start telling others
about the larger reality,
the scoffing and ridicule
can be heard for a hundred miles.

It's like trying to tell others about the Now.
They believe true liberty lives
only within the confines
of their own familiar borders.
They place it high atop a lofty pole,
then claim it's too high to reach.
A few realize it,
and step out forever from under
all the wind-driven flap.

Truly flying free,
their only anthem is silence.
They've forgotten how
to salute anything smaller
than the borderless freedom
they already are.

Sixty-Seven

An innocent looking gap
turns into a yawning chasm
that swallows the whole house.
A tiny split eventually tears
the entire table in two.

Beware of systems that make distinctions
between them and us,
good versus evil,
those who know,
and those who don't know.

Draw a line in the dirt
between *this* or *that*,
and you've already dug a trench
fertile for the seeds of war.

Sixty-Eight

A culture that profits from illness
will see fewer and fewer cures.
A country that profits from war
will see less and less of peace.

The two are interconnected.
The doctors fight disease
as if it were an enemy;
the soldiers fight the enemy
as if they were a disease.

The physician who treats
sickness as an enemy
is at war with health as well.

The commander who treats
other human beings
as a plague to be eradicated
is sick at heart himself.

Sixty-Nine

A true leader is like a master pruner.
He helps the people grow
by cutting back desires.
He knows limbs blossom
from the inside out.

So subtle is his technique,
no one can tell which branches
and vines he's trimmed.
The people flourish,
and the abundant harvest
is shared beyond the boundaries
of his own garden for miles.
In this way, he ensures that tools remain tools,
and don't get turned into weapons.

When visiting officials ask
what implements he uses,
his only response is the gently honed
glint of his smile.

No fertilizing with empty promises,
no hacking away at the people's spirit with fear,
he remains rooted in the Now,
keeps the overgrowth in check,
doesn't confuse economic strength
with true abundance,
recognizes an enemy as the offshoot
that naturally arises
out of the untended rot
within his own trees.

Seventy

The plum tree blossoms in winter,
despite harsh conditions.
The Master flowers as the Now
whether times are good or bad.

What tree, standing in the intense summer heat,
draws in its leaves, refusing others its shade?

What branch, come harvest,
pulls away, snatching back its fruit?

No mind, no mine.

Dropping bombs—
or dropping blossoms?

Seventy-One

In a culture that is soft,
the ego bursts like a soap bubble
when it's struck by the truth.

In a culture that is hard,
planes crashing into buildings
won't be enough.

To remain soft and supple,
the wise person lets go of all resistance,
lets go of resisting resisting,
lets go of letting go.

Start by noticing it in places
where you wouldn't normally notice it.
Start by looking for it in corners
where you'd rather not look:
religion, morality, democracy,
patriotism.

Its favorite line is,
and always has been:
Look! It's over there!

Seventy-Three

A mind-dominated culture
lives in past and future.
Mind-dominated industries
and technologies that thrive
on past and future
are the result.

How is this so?
Look inside your own house:
in drawers and closets,
on desktops and shelves,
yesterday's latest thing
has already been deemed passé
by the same minds that created it.
Tomorrow's version, model, design—
always new, always improved—
is now being touted as
the one you gotta have.

Weapons of mass distraction.
This is how the egoic self
fends off the present moment
that it fears.

Seventy-Four

Ten-thousand bigger-and-better shopping malls
cannot sell you your self. This is why,
no matter how many bags you fill,
sooner or later you feel empty.

That revved-up sports car
you keep lusting after? Forget it.
It will always arrive later
than what you already are.

I'm talking about your real face,
the one before Clinique
and Max Factor
and skin.

Look at you,
always making up who you are
out of that ridiculously tiny compact!

If only you could see
the vastness of your own truth
reflected between these words!

No mirror would ever
be large enough.

Seventy-Five

The upstairs neighbor's noisy.
The downstairs neighbor's quiet.
This is how it usually is,
even in the human being.

The solution?
Pack nothing.
Leave no forwarding address.
Move out from under the mind-made burden
of the self altogether, once and for all.
Otherwise, no matter where you relocate,
you'll still be living under the same tenant
and paying the same landlord.

Is the landlord bad? No.
He just can't imagine why
any thinking person would want
to live anywhere else.
He'd prefer that you
stay where you are,
rather than enter into
a new lease on life.

It's like this:
the heavy thought-baggage
you've been lugging around,
back and forth, from one concept-condo
to another all these years,
is completely empty when
you open it.

Seventy-Six

If all you do is think
your way through life,
then all you are in relationship to
are your own thoughts.

If all you do is judge others,
comparing them to yourself,
then the only person you are
in relationship to
is yourself.

If the only way you see the world
is through a veil of concepts,
beliefs, and ideas,
then the only thing
you are in relationship to
is your own mind.

What is enlightenment?
Realizing the truth of what you are
beyond thought,
and then embodying that.
Simply being life.

What is enlightened relationship?
Any relationship where Being,
rather than thinking,
is freely and consciously
meeting itself.

Seventy-Seven

Realizing the Now is like this:

people travel great distances
to the Grand Canyon
to gaze in awe at what isn't there.

Seventy-Eight

Stop trying to be loving,
and you are loving.
Stop trying to be compassionate,
and you are compassionate.

Trying *to be* anything involves the mind.
The mind involves separation—
this from that
other from self
self from the Now.

Separation and compassion are incompatible.
Who ever heard of trying to resuscitate
a dying man, mouth to mouth,
from thirty feet across the room?
At best, all you're doing is blowing
a lot of hot air around
about what you think compassion is:
sympathy, empathy, a kind of woolly we-ness;
but you aren't breathing new life
into anyone or anything.

Instead, loosen your thinking,
embrace simplicity,
relax your body and your gaze.

When the love you already are
becomes perfectly clear,
there is perfect self reflection.
When there is perfect self reflection,
you see your self everywhere
without a mirror in sight.

Seventy-Nine

The surest way to the heart of the Now
is to fall in love with it.

Make the present moment your lover.
Give it a lover's attention.
Step out of the dysfunctional
love-hate relationship you've been having
with life and the world.

Beneath the croon-woven coverlet of your skin
listen for the heartbeat that has no sound,
the pulse that is the heartthrob inside the pulse.
Press your lips to silence,
and let yourself be seduced by it.

Now, the entire cosmos is your bedroom,
and you don't even care who's watching!

When you swoon,
the universe swoons.

Eighty

The great spiritual falsehood?
That you have to wait until you die
to return to the Source.

The even greater falsehood?
That there's a you
separate from the Source
who needs to return at all.

Eighty-One

A primordial pool
of inexhaustible stillness,
from which everything arises
and to which everything returns,
rests beneath the surface of what
you call your real life
of noise and busyness,
desire and fear.

Beneath the continual need for noise
lies the fear of silence.
Beneath compulsive busyness:
the desire to feel truly alive.

This pool isn't muddied
by what happens on the surface.
When it wells up from the depths,
moments that lave you in the Now's
quiet clarity naturally appear.
Your mind will dismiss these,
but pay no attention.
Follow these moments
back to their Source,
back to that which is seeking
to know itself through you,
to know itself *as* you.

Realize this stillness to be what you are,
and you'll be at peace in the midst
of sorrow and upset,
level when surrounded
by chaos and imbalance,
watering the withered lives of beings
you don't know and will never,
in your lifetime, see.

ACKNOWLEDGEMENTS

The final quotation in Verse "Sixty-Five" was adapted from an interview with a Vietnam veteran that first appeared in *Street Roots*. The quotation from Sun Tzu in Verse "Sixty-Three" is from *A Little Book of Zen*, Andrews McMeel Publishing, Kansas City, 1998. Copyright Armand Eisen.

I pour out my heartfelt appreciation to the staff at the Portland Classical Chinese Garden/Tower of Cosmic Reflections teahouse who provided me with many sample refills while a number of these verses were being written. And to Gloria Lee, the Executive Director of the Portland Classical Chinese Garden, who graciously gave permission that the Garden's name might be used in this book. Thanks also to the many who make the gift of the Garden possible. It has been a source of inspiration, both to me and to countless others.

Like the tea-person in Verse "Forty-Three," thanks are also in order to those who have brought "what's been gathered on the heights down to where people can taste it." These include: teacher and writer Adyashanti; Stephen Mitchell, for his beautiful version of the *Tao Te Ching*; Eckhart Tolle, author of *The Power of Now*; the Taoist and Sufi Masters; and my former Tibetan Buddhist teacher Eric Marcoux, to whom Verse "Forty-Six" is dedicated. Your answer to my question: "But what about mystical union?" was the beginning of the end of everything.

To Randy and Leslie, my neighborhood computer support team. Thank you for loaning me your laptop when my thirteen-year-old Mac Performa 475 finally ascended to the big hard drive in the sky. Without you, this book would probably still be written down on pieces of paper and matchbook covers scattered around the house.

I bow to the beauty of Portland poet Paulann Petersen, former Stegner Fellow and Oregon Book Award poetry finalist for *A Bride of Narrow Escape*. Your tireless devotion to the Northwest literary community has made Oregon a poet's paradise.

Nearly twenty years ago, Naomi Shihab Nye's poetry somehow managed to find me in a Trappist monastery! Reading your work was like rediscovering a long-forgotten part of myself. Thank you for your support and "good cheer." Recognition and thanks are also in order to May Sarton, now deceased, whose work and communiqués helped me to taste the richness that solitude and silence have to offer. To the late Fr. Louis (Thomas) Merton, whose writings steered me in new, and entirely unforeseen directions. And with much gratitude in my heart for Oregon's late, great poet William Stafford, whose life and work embodied that to which this book can only point.

Good editors are like the Now. They personify the spaciousness within which a particular work comes into being. I'm thinking especially of Jennifer Bosveld, editor of *Pudding Magazine*, who has supported so much of my work over the past eighteen years. And to Ken Arnold and his wife Connie Kirk, whose dedication and enthusiasm made this book possible.

And finally, with love and gratitude to Ken.
Thank you for sharing the Now with me.

ABOUT THE AUTHOR

Daniel Skach-Mills was born in Coeur d'Alene, Idaho, and raised in Portland, Oregon. He holds an undergraduate degree from Marylhurst University, Marylhurst, Oregon; and a graduate degree from St. Martin's University in Lacey, Washington. His award-winning poetry has appeared in a variety of publications and anthologies, including: *The Christian Science Monitor, The Christian Century, Sojourners, Open Spaces,* and *Prayers To Protest: Poems That Center And Bless Us* (Pudding House Publications, 1998). His chapbook, *Gold: Daniel Skach-Mills's Greatest Hits, 1990-2000*, appeared in 2001 from Pudding House.

He has been a featured reader in the Northwest for events at Looking Glass Bookstore, Marylhurst University, Living Earth Gatherings, KBOO Radio, and The Friends of William Stafford. A psychotherapist and spiritual teacher, he has lived both as a Benedictine and a Trappist monk, and is currently a volunteer docent for Lan Su Chinese Garden. He and his partner live in Portland, Oregon.

CPSIA information can be obtained at www.ICGtesting.com
Printed in the USA
BVOW06s0830020116

431607BV00039B/927/P

Seventy-Two

Disney evil is easy.
That's why people like it.

Real evil is hard to see.
That's because of the wide brim
on the white ten-gallon hat
it keeps pulling down
over people's eyes.

Lose touch with the formless,
and the ability to see yourself as other
and the other as yourself
disintegrates.

This is when evil appears.

Launch a crusade against it,
rather than replacing it
with awareness of the Now,
and you commit evil yourself.